MILESTONES
IN MODERN SCIENCE

THE DISCOVERY OF
PENICILLIN

Guy de la Bédoyère

Evans

Published by Evans Brothers Limited
2A Portman Mansions
Chiltern Street
London W1U 6NR

© Evans Brothers Limited 2005

First published 2005

British Library Cataloguing in Publication Data

De la Bedoyere, Guy
The discovery of penicillin. - (Milestones in modern science)
  1. Penicillin - History - Juvenile literature
  2. Discoveries in science - Juvenile literature
  I. Title
615. 3' 923

ISBN 0237527391

Consultant: Dr Anne Whitehead
Editor: Sonya Newland
Designer: D.R. Ink, info@d-r-ink.com
Picture researcher: Julia Bird

Acknowledgements

Cover St Mary's Hospital/Science Photo Library; © Bettmann/Corbis; John Durham/Science Photo Library 3 National Museum of Photography, Film & Television/Daily Herald Archive/Science & Society Picture Library 4 Sotiris Zafeiris/Science Photo Library 5 Science Museum/Science & Society Picture Library 6 Andrew Syred/Science Photo Library 8 Tony Craddock/Science Photo Library 9(t) Gusto/Science Photo Library 9(b) Rosenfeld Images Ltd/Science Photo Library 10 Sinclair Stammers/Science Photo Library 11(l) Alfred Pasieka/Science Photo Library 11(r) David Scharf/Science Photo Library 12(r) Dr L. Stannard, UCT/Science Photo Library 13(b) Science Museum/Science & Society Picture Library 14(t) Volker Steger, Peter Arnold Inc./Science Photo Library 14(b) Dr Jeremy Burgess/Science Photo Library 15(l) Science Photo Library 15(r) Eye of Science/Science Photo Library 16(t) Science Museum/Science & Society Picture Library 16(b) Science Photo Library 17 National Museum of Photography, Film & Television/Science & Society Picture Library 18(t) Laguna Design/Science Photo Library 18(b) Science Photo Library 19(t) Science Photo Library 19(b) National Museum of Photography, Film & Television/Daily Herald Archive/Science & Society Picture Library 20(t) Div. Of Computer Research & Technology, National Institute of Health/Science Photo Library 20(b) St Mary's Hospital/Science Photo Library 21(t) Kwangshin Kim/Science Photo Library 21(b) CNRI/Science Photo Library 22 © Bettmann/Corbis 23 Science Photo Library 24 National Museum of Photography, Film & Television/Daily Herald Archive/Science & Society Picture Library 25(t) © Hulton-Deutsch Collection/Corbis 25(b) Science Museum/Science & Society Picture Library 26(b) © Bettmann/Corbis 26-27 National Museum of Photography, Film & Television/Daily Herald Archive/Science & Society Picture Library 27(b) National Museum of Photography, Film & Television/Daily Herald Archive/Science & Society Picture Library 28 National Museum of Photography, Film & Television/Daily Herald Archive/Science & Society Picture Library 29 Science Photo Library 30(t) National Museum of Photography, Film & Television/Daily Herald Archive/Science & Society Picture Library 30(b) National Museum of Photography, Film & Television/Daily Herald Archive/Science & Society Picture Library 31 Manchester Daily Express/Science & Society Picture Library 32(t) National Museum of Photography, Film & Television/Daily Herald Archive/Science & Society Picture Library 32(b) Dr Jeremy Burgess/Science Photo Library 33 Science Museum/Science & Society Picture Library 34 © Bettmann/Corbis 35(t) Michael Abbey/Science Photo Library 35(b) Science Museum/Science & Society Picture Library 36(t) Dr Gopal Murti/Science Photo Library 36(b) John Durham/Science Photo Library 37(r) Dr Kari Lounatmaa/Science Photo Library 38(t) Kenneth Eward/Biografx/Science Photo Library 38(b) Princess Margaret Rose Orthopaedic Hospital/Science Photo Library 39 Dr Kari Lounatmaa/Science Photo Library 40(t) John Walsh/Science Photo Library 40(b) BSIP, Laurent/Science Photo Library 41(m) Eye of Science/Science Photo Library 41(b) Josh Sher/Science Photo Library 42 John McLean/Science Photo Library 43 Sinclair Stammers/Science Photo Library 44 John Durham/Science Photo Library

CONTENTS

'*Once a clue has been obtained, teamwork may be absolutely necessary to bring the discovery to full advantage.*' ALEXANDER FLEMING

Introduction

ABOVE: *Today, methods of carrying out research into bacteria are not so different from in Fleming's time. This plate shows the jelly-like agar (red), with several types of bacteria (green and brown). The white bit in the middle is a mould.*

The discovery of penicillin was one of the most important advances in the history of medical science – and it began with a mistake. The scientist Alexander Fleming was researching bacteria; in September 1928 he went off on holiday for a few days without clearing up the glass plates on which he had placed some of the bacteria. When he returned to his laboratory, he noticed that one of these glass plates had a mould growing on it. In itself this was not unusual, but something about this particular mould caught Fleming's eye. All around it there was a ring that seemed to be free of the bacteria. Bacteria are the cause of many diseases, and in the course of his research Fleming had started to wonder how they might be killed. He realised that this mould – *Penicillium* – must contain a substance that could do just that. He called it penicillin. It was lucky that Fleming was not a tidy man, and equally lucky that he realised the significance of what he saw that day.

Other scientists, including Howard Florey and Ernst Chain, took up the investigation into penicillin, and began to search for ways to make it widely available. There was a great need for it by this time, because the Second World War was raging and soldiers were dying in their thousands from infected wounds that army doctors simply could not treat. A team of British and American scientists finally hit upon a way of producing enough penicillin to help everyone, and towards the end of the war soldiers were even provided with their own penicillin kits.

In the second half of the twentieth century, other bacteria-killing substances were found that could treat many types of infectious diseases. These became known collectively as antibiotics. People thought pencillin and other antibiotics were wonder-drugs and they grew to be some of the most widely used prescriptions in the western world.

As time went on, however, scientists and doctors discovered some problems with using penicillin. Because bacteria can change rapidly and adapt to new conditions, they were able to evolve into forms that antibiotics could not treat. Also, it was a long time before people realised that a full and accurate dose of penicillin must be taken in order to be effective. Even when patients feel better, not all the bacteria may have been killed and the infection can quickly return if the complete course is not taken. Despite the problems, penicillin-based antibiotics are still considered to be the safest in medicine, although scientists continue to research other ways of killing bacteria. Since penicillin first became available in the 1940s it has undoubtedly saved thousands – possibly millions – of lives, and today it is difficult to imagine our world without it.

ABOVE: *A sample of* Penicillium *mould from one of Alexander Fleming's experiments in 1935. It has been preserved and mounted – demonstrating just how important Fleming's discovery of the mould's bacteria-killing qualities is believed to be.*

CHAPTER ONE

'I had a clue that here was something good, but I could not possibly know how good it was.' ALEXANDER FLEMING

Bacteria and Disease

ABOVE: *These rod-shaped bacteria – magnified to 21,500 times their actual size – are E-coli, which live in the intestine and are usually harmless. If they increase in number or break through the intestinal wall, however, they can cause infection.*

Fact

DNA AND RNA

DNA (deoxyribonucleic acid) is what tells a cell how to feed, grow, reproduce, excrete, move and respond to the environment. The information in DNA is translated by RNA (ribonucleic acid) into instructions that tell the cell how to make proteins, which are an essential component of all organisms.

NOT ALL BACTERIA ARE BAD, BUT THERE are many that cause different infections and diseases, ranging from food poisoning to life-threatening illnesses such as meningitis. The discovery of a substance that could kill bacteria, therefore, was a giant leap forward in medical science. To fully understand why the discovery was so important and why it took so long for penicillin to become widely available, it is important to understand a few things about the nature of bacteria and disease.

PLANT AND ANIMAL CELLS

Every living thing, whether plant, animal or bacterium, is made from cells. Human beings are made of billions of cells, but simple animals are made from only a few. Each cell can live by itself and has a skin, or membrane, that holds it together. Cells are generally extremely small, but some can be seen with the naked eye – perhaps as big as the full stop at the end of this sentence.

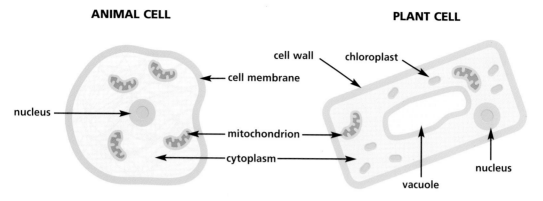

ANIMAL CELL

PLANT CELL

cell wall — chloroplast

cell membrane

nucleus

mitochondrion

cytoplasm

nucleus

vacuole

Plant and animal cells 'know' where they belong and what they have to do, because each cell contains a nucleus, which controls how the cell works. Around the nucleus is a jelly-like material called cytoplasm.

All living organisms have DNA. Plant and animal cells are called 'eukaryotic' organisms, because their cells have a definite nucleus containing DNA. A gene is a length of DNA that controls what the body looks like and how it responds to disease. Chains of thousands of genes form chromosomes. Normal human cells each have 46 chromosomes and about 60,000 genes.

WHAT ARE BACTERIA?

The word 'bacterium' comes from the Greek word *bakterion*, meaning 'small rod', because some types take this shape. Bacteria are single-celled organisms that are found everywhere on Earth. Unlike plant and animal cells, they do not have nuclei. Their genetic information is found in a single filament of DNA, in a chromosome called the nucleoid or in plasmids (see p. 8). Cells like this are called 'prokaryotic'. Bacteria have thousands of genes, and structures called ribosomes that make protein. They move around using the flagellum.

ABOVE: *Plant and animal cells have some differences. For example, plant cells usually have regular shapes, while animal cells are irregular; plant cells contain chloroplast (which controls colour) and a vacuole – a cavity filled with fluid. Both have DNA in their nuclei, which contains all the information the cells need to grow and reproduce. They also both have mitochondria, the power house of the cell.*

BELOW: *A typical bacterium cell.*

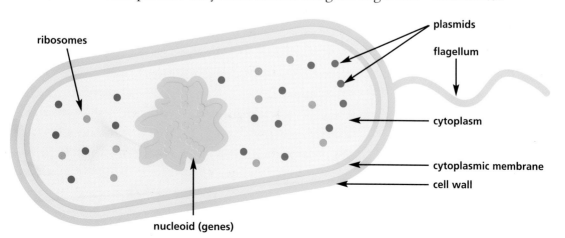

ribosomes

plasmids

flagellum

cytoplasm

cytoplasmic membrane

cell wall

nucleoid (genes)

Because of the frequency with which they reproduce, bacteria can mutate into new forms very quickly. This means they can adapt rapidly to new conditions, creating forms that can live almost anywhere, even in places like deep-sea vents, where the temperature can reach 300°C. New types of bacteria are being found all the time.

ABOVE: *Bacteria can survive even in very high temperatures. The different colour graduations in this hot pool in Yellowstone National Park, Wyoming, USA, indicate different bacteria living in different temperature zones.*

Fact

GOOD AND BAD BACTERIA
Bacteria in the human body fall into two groups: normal and invaders. Normal bacteria are those that exist in the body all the time. These rarely cause disease and can even be beneficial. Invaders are bacteria that find their way into the body through the air or contaminated food. These are the bacteria that often cause disease.

Some bacteria have additional DNA carried by plasmids (see diagram on p. 7). Plasmids can reproduce independently and be passed from one bacterium to another, including those of different species, in a process called conjugation. Plasmids are very important because they often contain the genes that are used to help the bacterium fight off anything that might threaten it – this even includes the antibiotics used to fight bacteria.

WHAT DO BACTERIA DO?

The word 'bacteria' often makes people think of illness and dirt, but it is important to remember that not all bacteria are harmful. All animals, including humans, have bacteria in their guts that help them to digest their food. These bacteria have a symbiotic relationship, that is, both parties benefit: the bacteria get food and water, and the animal gets those vitamins that are made available by the bacteria. They can also be a very important part of the natural world. Some bacteria break down plant matter like leaves in the autumn to

Fact

TYPES OF BACTERIA

The different types of bacteria are recognised by their shapes.

ACTINOMYCETES
thread-like

BACILLI
shaped like rods

COCCI
round in shape

COCCOBACILLI
oval in shape

IRREGULAR
without a defined shape

SPIRILLA
rigid spiral-shaped

SPIROCHAETES
flexible spiral-shaped

VIBRIOS
shaped like commas

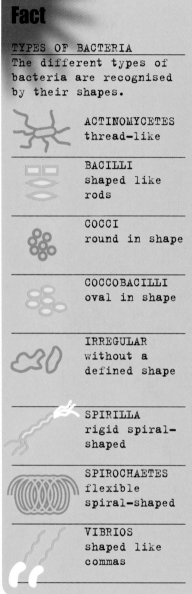

make substances called nitrates, which are used as fertilisers. Other bacteria grow on the roots of plants and convert nitrogen in the air and soil into nitrates. Plants, including food crops, need these nitrates in order to grow. Still other types of bacteria are used to help make foods like cheese and yoghurt.

ABOVE: Compost is made of decaying kitchen and garden waste. The bacteria in the compost break down the waste, creating nitrates, which are good soil fertilisers.

LEFT: Yoghurt is matured in incubation tanks like these by adding cultures of specific bacteria to milk.

WHAT CAUSES DISEASE?

A disease is a condition that stops a living organism from working normally. It may affect the whole organism or just part of it, for example, an organ in the human body or one of its systems like the blood supply.

Doctors and scientists can usually tell one disease from another by the symptoms it causes. Symptoms are signs of things going wrong – for example, a high temperature, or when an organ such as a kidney stops working. For hundreds of years, scientists have been trying to find out what causes diseases so that they can prevent and cure them.

Today scientists know that one of many causes of disease is infection. Our bodies are under constant attack by micro-organisms, which usually find their way in through our mouths in food or even just the air we breathe. Micro-organisms also enter through wounds in the skin. This might be from an injury, during an operation in hospital or through an insect bite.

There are many different types of micro-organism that can cause disease. The two most significant are bacteria and viruses. Some bacteria can survive independently, while others need to live as parasites – inside or on another living organism. Viruses are smaller infectious agents that can only live and reproduce within the cells of other living things.

Although bacteria can be found almost anywhere, they thrive in warm, damp conditions. The human mouth, nose and intestine are ideal places for bacteria to live and reproduce.

Most bacteria are harmless. Those that cause disease are called pathogens. There is always the possibility of being infected by pathogens because they are around us all the time. The bacteria reproduce in the human gut and create poisons that can make a person feel ill and cause a rise in body temperature. Humans and animals that are ill may have the disease-causing bacteria in their saliva or in the mucus in their noses.

Fact

BACTERIAL REPRODUCTION
All cells normally reproduce by dividing into two. This process is called binary fission. Some bacteria do this every 20 minutes. This means that one bacterium can generate 2,097,152 bacteria in just seven hours. After another hour the total can rise to a staggering 16,777,216. With a rate of reproduction like this, there are more bacteria in 30 cm of your gut than there are people on Earth.

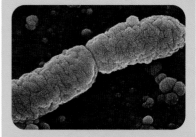

ABOVE: A bacterium undergoing binary fission. This method of reproduction is used by a bacterium to produce a genetically and structurally identical clone, or daughter cell.

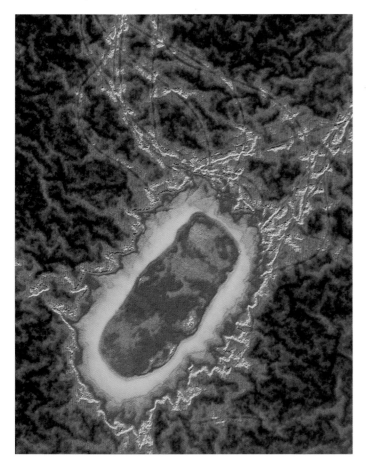

LEFT: Pathogens are bacteria that cause disease. This coloured image shows a single salmonella bacterium, magnified 21,000 times. These bacteria can cause food poisoning if enough of them are present on contaminated food. Symptoms include nausea, vomiting and diarrhoea.

When they cough or sneeze, the bacteria are sent out into the air in tiny droplets of saliva or mucus. People or animals nearby who breathe in the droplets may catch the same disease.

As well as bacteria that get into our bodies from outside, there are also bacteria already inside us. Our intestines have many bacteria living in them. These normally cause no harm because the intestinal wall stops them from getting to other parts of the body. In a similar way, we have a protective membrane in our noses, which usually prevents bacteria from transferring to other parts of the body. Sometimes these bacteria break through their protective barriers, though, and this is when they can cause infection.

RIGHT: *The large green and blue circles in this picture are hepatitis B viruses. The smaller circles and the rods are antigens, which are used to make vaccines against the disease.*

BELOW: *Some white blood cells, found in the immune system, destroy bacteria by surrounding, engulfing and digesting them. These are known as 'phagocytes'.*

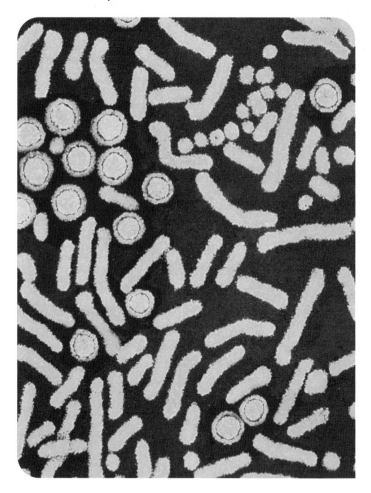

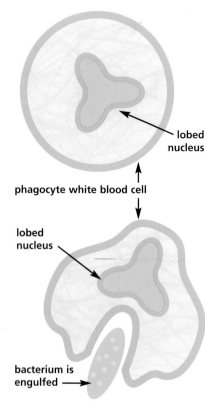

lobed
nucleus

phagocyte white blood cell

lobed
nucleus

bacterium is
engulfed

NATURAL DEFENCES AGAINST BACTERIA

Even if a pathogen does get inside the body, it will not necessarily cause an infection. Microbes, including bacteria, have proteins known as antigens, and each antigen is unique to each bacterium. White blood cells can recognise an individual antigen. They make antibodies that will attack and often destroy the

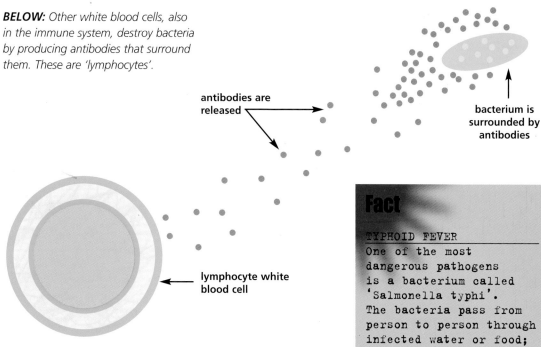

BELOW: Other white blood cells, also in the immune system, destroy bacteria by producing antibodies that surround them. These are 'lymphocytes'.

antibodies are released

bacterium is surrounded by antibodies

lymphocyte white blood cell

pathogen. They also 'remember' that particular antigen, so if those bacteria ever get inside the body again, the white blood cells are ready with antibodies.

But pathogens are equipped to fight back, and some are either too numerous to be destroyed before they start causing disease, or they destroy the white blood cells. These pathogens then release their poisons. In these cases, infection or disease results.

Fact

TYPHOID FEVER
One of the most dangerous pathogens is a bacterium called 'Salmonella typhi'. The bacteria pass from person to person through infected water or food; they can also be carried by flies. People who are infected develop typhoid fever. The result is a severe infection of the bowel, causing bleeding. About one in ten people who catch it die. Until antibiotics were dis-covered, the disease was almost untreatable.

Key People

Prince Albert (1819–61), Queen Victoria's husband, was a gifted and intelligent man. He was interested in new discoveries in the areas of science and medicine. He promoted the Great Exhibition of 1851, at which countries from all around the world displayed new inventions. In 1861 he caught typhoid fever. In the nineteenth century, nobody had any idea what caused the disease and no idea how to treat it, and so Prince Albert died. Typhoid killed rich and poor alike, and it was very common until about 1900 in large cities where a contaminated water supply could infect hundreds of people. Victoria and Albert's son later caught typhoid fever, but survived.

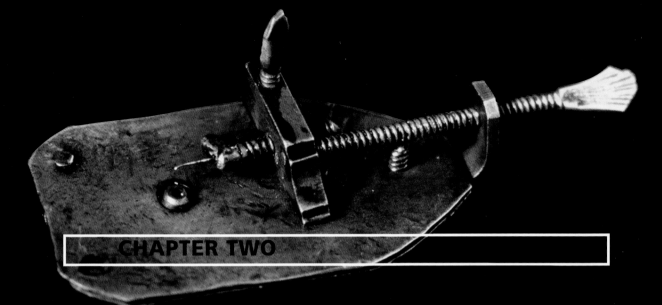

CHAPTER TWO

'My only merit is that I did not neglect the observation and that I pursued the subject as a bacteriologist.' **ALEXANDER FLEMING**

The Path to Penicillin

ABOVE: *An early microscope, made by Anton van Leeuwenhoek. The lens was clamped between two brass plates with holes to look through, and the specimen was placed on the tip of the needle. It was only about 8 cm long and magnified the specimen 200 times.*

BELOW: *Van Leeuwenhoek's diagrams of 'animalcules'.*

THE FIRST OBSERVATION OF BACTERIA was made in 1683 by the Dutch scientist Anton van Leeuwenhoek (1632–1723). Using microscopes he had made himself, he examined plaque in his own teeth, and described the 'animalcules' he saw moving about. He was amazed at how many there were and the ways in which they moved about. But he could not explain what they were or what purpose they served. Some of the things he saw were bacteria, but it was more than 150 years before people realised that they could cause disease.

LIFE IN THE NINETEENTH CENTURY

During the nineteenth century trade and industry were on the increase. Nations like Great Britain and the United States were growing richer. In 1750 London had a population of 650,000. By 1851 it had risen to nearly 2.5 million. In the USA, Chicago's population leaped from 3,000 in the 1830s to nearly 110,000 in 1860. By 1900 it was home to around 1.7 million people.

People flocked to the cities to work in factories, and they became overcrowded. Whole families often lived in single rooms in small houses and in filthy conditions. This meant that disease and infection spread easily. People arriving from the countryside were exposed to new diseases and brought in diseases of their own that they passed on. As international trade grew, diseases were spread around the world on ships. This was how cholera eventually reached the West from India in the 1800s, and the disease quickly reached epidemic proportions in several of the most built-up areas of Britain. Investigations into the cause of cholera were the first steps on the path to the discovery of penicillin.

Although people knew that unhygienic living conditions could spread disease, they did not know why. In the cities, there was no way of getting fresh,

Fact

THE PUBLIC HEALTH ACT, 1848

Governments grew increasingly concerned about the spread of infection, and were worried that epidemics might cause riots or public disorder. After a cholera outbreak in 1847–48, the Public Health Act was passed in England. This set up a central Board of Health, and made local councils responsible for issues such as drainage and water supplies. Taxes were raised to help pay for these improvements.

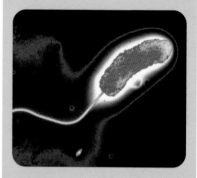

ABOVE: The bacterium that causes cholera, Vibrio cholerae, is an example of a comma-shaped bacterium. It is a water-borne pathogen and can be transmitted to humans through contaminated water.

LEFT: Cities like Exeter (pictured here in the 1830s) were overcrowded and conditions were unhygienic. People washed their clothes in the rivers that supplied drinking water, and there was no way of recycling and purifying the water as there is today.

ABOVE: *Louis Pasteur, who conducted experiments that proved micro-organisms could cause decay and disease, rather than being produced during the decaying process, as many people had previously thought.*

clean water and virtually no system for removing dirty water. Sewage and rubbish lay in the streets where children played and where people collected water from water-pumps. The water was contaminated with faeces and contained bacteria and viruses. Since no one knew micro-organisms existed, let alone what they did, disease was rife. Many babies and small children died. Life expectancy was low – few people lived past the age of 45.

FINDING THE CAUSE OF DISEASE

In 1796 Edward Jenner had shown that the disease smallpox could be controlled by a process of vaccination, in which a very low dosage of the virus that caused the disease was injected into a healthy person. It was not enough to make the person ill, but just enough that the white blood cells in the body recognised the antigens and made antibodies to fight it in case it appeared again (see p. 12). Ever since this time, the race had been on to find vaccines for other diseases and new methods of preventing infection.

Louis Pasteur (1822–95) was a French scientist who made the great discovery in 1861 that micro-organisms cause food to decay. Pasteur put boiled milk, beer and wine into special sealed containers.

Key People

John Snow (1813–58), an English doctor, suggested that cholera was caught from contaminated food or water rather than being breathed in, as people generally believed. In 1854 a cholera epidemic broke out in London. Snow made a record of where the worst cases occurred, and found that a large number of people affected took their water from a single pump, situated where two streets joined. Snow removed the handle to stop people using this particular pump and almost immediately new cases of cholera were drastically reduced. Snow's work is recognised as one of the first great pieces of medical research into identifying the source of a disease. However, he could still not explain what it was in the water that had caused the cholera.

Fact

WAR AND EPIDEMIC

Between 1861 and 1865 the American Civil War raged between the northern and southern states. The casualties were very high; around 620,000 soldiers died during the war. Of these, almost two-thirds were killed not on the battlefields, but by disease. Men from remote farms came into contact with crowds of other men, and they caught diseases from one another. The filthy conditions in which they had to live allowed bacteria and viruses to multiply and pass between the soldiers. Battlefield injuries became infected and because there was no treatment for such infections, soldiers often died.

RIGHT: Medical provisions were lacking during the American Civil War. Soldiers were treated in filthy tents with no hygiene standards, and infections spread rapidly.

The wine and beer did not ferment and the milk did not go sour. When he removed the seals and allowed micro-organisms in, the wine and beer fermented and the milk went sour. Until Pasteur's discovery, many scientists had believed that micro-organisms were produced when substances went rotten. Pasteur had proved that some micro-organisms actually cause disease and decay.

IDENTIFYING TYPES OF BACTERIA

The next step was to identify which bacterium caused which disease. A sample taken from a patient with cholera or tuberculosis had many different bacteria in it. To try to relate certain bacteria to specific diseases, the German scientist Dr Robert Koch (1843–1910) took a sample and spread it on agar, a kind of solid jelly on which bacteria can grow. The different types of bacteria grew in their own colonies. By taking lots of samples from different patients suffering from the same disease, he could identify the one that was associated with the disease. In 1883 Koch finally found the cholera bacterium. He also identified the bacteria that cause tuberculosis and anthrax, both common and often deadly diseases at the time. Koch helped to pioneer the idea of improved hygiene as a way of preventing diseases. Once again, this was a huge step in the right direction. However, it was one thing to prevent disease by bacterial infection, but quite another to kill the bacteria in people who had already been infected.

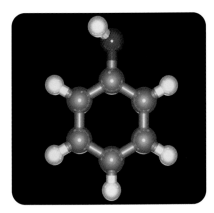

ABOVE: *The molecular structure of the antibacterial agent phenol, used by Joseph Lister to kill bacteria on wounds. It is made up of carbon (blue), hydrogen (white) and oxygen (red). On its own, phenol could also destroy living tissue, so it was quite dangerous to use.*

THE SEARCH FOR ANTIBACTERIAL SUBSTANCES

There are several ways of killing bacteria. Most are killed by being exposed to temperatures above boiling or ultraviolet light. Bacterial reproduction can be slowed down by cold, but this rarely kills them. Boiling and ultraviolet light kill almost all bacteria, but many bacteria serve a useful purpose in the human body. Doctors and scientists needed to find a way of killing invading bacteria that could cause disease, without killing the normal bacteria.

Influenced by Pasteur's work, an English surgeon, Sir Joseph Lister (1827–1912), pioneered the use of chemical antiseptics, such as phenol, to kill bacteria on operating equipment and on wounds. This was a great advance, but while phenol and other antiseptics could sterilise medical implements and kill bacteria on the surface of the body, they could not be used internally because they could harm or even kill the patient.

Fact

EARLIER DISCOVERIES OF PENICILLIN

★ John Tyndall had observed how a species of 'Penicillium' mould had killed bacteria in 1876 during his own experiments.

★ 'Penicillium' mould was first found by a scientist called Richard Westling in 1911, on the hyssop plant in Norway.

★ In 1925, just a few years before Fleming's own research, André Gratia and Sarah Dath found that the mould killed a bacteria known as 'Staphylococcus' on their culture plates. They published their discovery, but no one took any notice.

ABOVE: *John Tyndall giving a scientific lecture in London in 1870. He was the first person to notice that mould from the Penicillium family killed bacteria.*

Key People

Paul Ehrlich (1854–1915), a German biologist, had worked as an assistant to Robert Koch (see p. 17). Ehrlich was also a pioneer in identifying bacteria and finding drugs that targeted individual diseases. He called these drugs 'magic bullets', because they only killed exactly what they were supposed to. By 1909 he had developed a drug based on arsenic called salvarsan, which killed the bacteria that caused syphilis. Salvarsan became the basis of many other disease-treating drugs.

FLEMING'S LUCKY BREAK

Then along came Alexander Fleming (1881–1955) – the man credited with discovering penicillin. Fleming was a scientist with a special interest in bacteria and disease, and he was looking for a substance that would slow the growth of bacteria.

One day in 1921 Fleming was suffering from a cold. While at work in his laboratory, some of his nasal mucus dripped on to one of the culture dishes.

LEFT: *Alexander Fleming in his laboratory with a collection of mould cultures, during his research into bacteria in the 1920s.*

RIGHT: This computer-generated image shows the antibacterial enzyme lysozyme, discovered by Fleming in 1921. Lysozyme works by breaking down the cell walls of bacteria, making it easier for them to be destroyed.

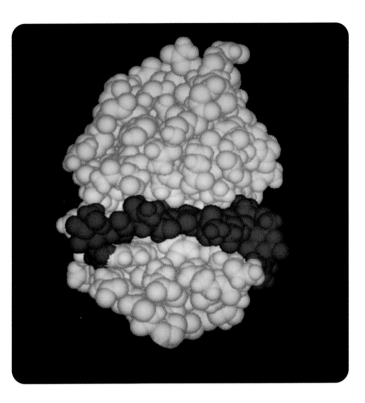

BELOW: After noticing that the bacteria around the mould on his culture dish had been killed, Fleming carefully recorded what it looked like so he could try to recreate the same results – this time on purpose!

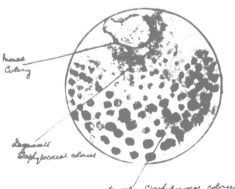

Fleming noticed that the bacteria around the mucus was killed. He conducted further tests by preparing mucus samples with a common bacterium, *Staphylococcus*, for examination. In each trial, the bacteria around the mucus was killed. Fleming now knew that mucus from the human nose could kill some types of bacteria, and he correctly deduced from this that nature produced its own bacteria-killing substances. He called this substance 'lysozyme', and further research showed that it was present in many different fluids, including human tears and even egg white. Unfortunately, lysozyme was not very effective at wiping out disease-causing bacteria, so Fleming continued his search.

Several years later, in September 1928, Fleming laid out culture plates with samples just before going on holiday. When he returned he found, to his surprise, that a mould had grown on one of the samples. All around the mould there were no bacteria.

Moulds are fungi, related to mushrooms. They do not produce seeds. Instead they send reproductive

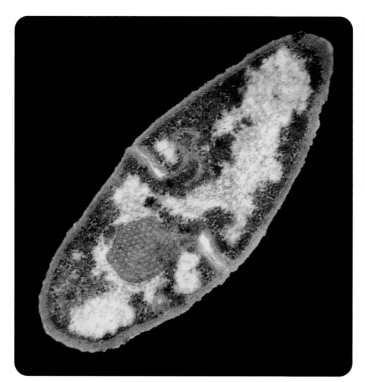

LEFT: Diphtheria *bacteria (shown here
magnified 25,000 times) were among
the first to be treated with penicillin.
They are rod-shaped and multiply
rapidly once inside the body. Today,
vaccination means that the disease
diphtheria is rare in the West.*

particles called spores into the air, where they drift
about. Those that land on suitable food start to grow –
and that is exactly what had happened in Fleming's
laboratory while he was away and the culture plate was
left untouched. It was a stroke of luck.

Fact

WHY DID IT HAPPEN?

When other researchers tried to recreate
Fleming's discovery, they found they could
not do it – the mould would not grow. One
of Fleming's assistants, Ronald Hare, found
out why, and it showed what a lucky chance
Fleming's discovery had been. The bacteria
Fleming had been studying and which had been
left on the culture dish were 'Staphylococcus',
which grow best at 35°C. 'Penicillium' mould
grows better in cooler conditions, around
20°C. When Fleming was on holiday, the
temperature had been unusually cool, allowing
the penicillin to grow first. When the air
warmed up and the 'Staphylococcus' started
growing, the penicillin was already present.

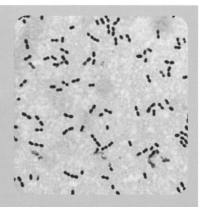

ABOVE: Streptococcus *bacteria
are rounded and often appear in
chains of three or four. Fleming's
experiments proved that penicillin
could kill this type of bacteria.*

ABOVE: *Fleming (pictured in his laboratory at St Mary's Hospital, London, around 1929) used penicillin as a means of identifying bacteria rather than as a treatment for infection – it was too difficult to produce in large quantities to be really useful in medicine. Or so he believed.*

Fleming realised that something in the mould had killed the bacteria next to it. The mould was *Penicillium notatum*, so Fleming named its bacteria-killing chemical 'penicillin'. Later, scientists discovered that penicillin works by stopping the bacteria making cells walls, which means that they cannot divide and multiply. They stretch out, and eventually the cell wall becomes so weak that it bursts, and the bacteria are destroyed.

Fleming tried further experiments. He put his penicillin on one culture plate and lysozyme on another, and then put several different types of bacteria on each culture. He was astonished to see that, unlike lysozyme, his new discovery had a dramatic effect on disease-causing bacteria like *Streptococcus* and *Staphylococcus*. However, it didn't work on everything. For example, the bacteria that cause cholera and typhoid fever were unaffected.

PROBLEMS WITH PENICILLIN

In 1929, Fleming published his findings. Even after his discovery became known, however, there was no immediate chance of it being used to treat people. *Penicillium notatum* was very difficult to grow, and producing large quantities was impossible at that time.

Fleming found that the human body did not absorb his form of penicillin if it was taken orally. Even penicillin that was injected directly into the body soon passed out in urine. Fleming found that penicillin was very difficult to make and easily destroyed.

Fleming believed *Penicillium notatum* was more useful in helping to identify the bacteria that cause diseases than in treating them. He used penicillin to kill bacteria he did not want, so that he could research bacteria he was interested in, for example, the one that caused whooping cough (*pertussis*). He continued to make and use penicillin but he grew more interested in new drugs, sulphonamides – chemicals based on a substance called sulphanilamide – that were known to kill bacteria.

Fleming left a very important legacy, however: he had preserved cultures of penicillin and published his work. New researchers could continue his investigations.

Fact

HOW SULPHONAMIDES WORK

Sulphonamide drugs work by tricking bacteria. Bacteria need a growth substance, para-aminobenzoic acid, and are fooled into thinking the sulphonamide drug is this. They feed on it and are poisoned. Sulphonamide drugs were soon found to be very useful in killing bacteria that cause several diseases, including pneumonia and meningitis.

Key People

Gerhard Domagk (1895–1964) was a German scientist who discovered sulphonamides. While investigating sulphanilamide, he found that it killed bacteria. His experiments on animals showed that sulphonamide protected them against doses of bacteria that would normally be lethal. In 1935 he successfully treated his own daughter, who had streptococcal septicaemia. This led to the first antibacterial drugs that could be taken orally, and they ended up saving millions of lives. Domagk received the Nobel Prize for Medicine in 1939.

CHAPTER THREE

'*What's the patient like? Is he doing well? Oh, that's marvellous isn't it?*' ERNST CHAIN DURING THE ALEXANDER TRIAL

Making Penicillin Work

PENICILLIN'S BACTERIA-KILLING QUALITIES HAD BEEN DISCOVERED, but Fleming had thought it was too difficult and expensive to produce in effective quantities, and had all but abandoned his research into it. It was now up to other scientists to take the discovery further. The two that led the way were Howard Florey and Ernst Chain.

ABOVE: *These tiny bottles contain small amounts of penicillin; once Florey and Chain had proved penicillin's effectiveness they faced an even bigger challenge – producing it on a large scale, so that it could be used to help the thousands of injured soldiers in the Second World War.*

THE ISOLATION OF PENICILLIN

In 1938, a man called Howard Florey was in charge of a team of researchers at the William Dunn School of Pathology at Oxford University. They had been fascinated by Domagk's discovery of suphonamides, and hoped to find other moulds that could kill bacteria. *Penicillium notatum* was one of the moulds the Oxford team researched. Why did they choose this? One of the possible reasons is a chance conversation Florey is reported to have had with Dr Cecil Paine several years earlier. Paine's interest had been sparked by reading one of Fleming's papers about penicillin, and he had learned to make a crude form of it himself. He wanted to try it out. A miner had come to see him with a stone stuck in his eye. The stone had caused a very

Key People

Ernst Chain (1906–79) was a German Jewish chemist. He was researching enzymes in Berlin when Hitler's National Socialist (Nazi) Party came to power in 1933. Chain realised that things were going to become very bad for Jewish people in Germany, so he emigrated to England. In 1935 he joined the William Dunn School of Pathology in Oxford. In 1938 he started work on penicillin with Howard Florey. After sharing the Nobel Prize for Medicine with Fleming and Florey in 1945, he continued his work on antibiotics and penicillin, and also began researching insulin.

serious infection and the miner was due to have an operation to have his eye removed. Paine decided to try his penicillin and see if it cleared the infection. It worked, and the miner's eye was saved. Paine never published his findings – he felt that his penicillin extract was too crude to be taken seriously and that more research was needed. Other work distracted him, however, and it was only when he mentioned his experiment to Florey that someone picked up where he had left off.

Ernst Chain was a key member of Florey's Oxford team, and was responsible for most of the actual research. He was fascinated by Fleming's work and used one of Fleming's original penicillin cultures to experiment on. Although he was intrigued by what penicillin could do, he was not setting out to find a miracle cure – penicillin was still far too difficult to make and use. However, during his experiments, Chain managed to

ABOVE: Early penicillin-making apparatus; the box on the left was used for fermentation. The bottles show the results of early experiments.

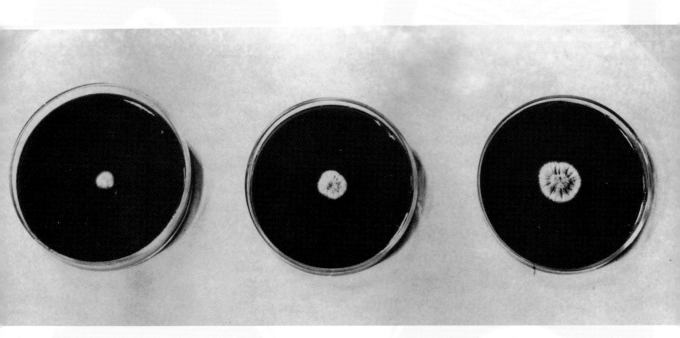

ABOVE: *These penicillin cultures were made in 1943. The petri dishes contain bacteria (the dark background in each dish). The lighter dot in the middle is the mould spore, which grows larger across the page. The white ring around the outside of the mould is the area where bacteria has been killed.*

make penicillin that was purer than anything Fleming had produced. The next thing to do was to try it out.

However, Chain needed Florey's permission to conduct experiments on animals. He showed Florey his results, and asked him to authorise further research – testing the penicillin on mice. Florey would not agree, however, and even accused Chain of pestering him. When Florey went on holiday, Chain persuaded another member of the team, J. M. Barnes, to try the penicillin out. Barnes injected two mice

RIGHT: *Ernst Chain (photographed in London in 1944) made a purer form of penicillin than Fleming had created. He had to conduct his first experiments on mice secretly, but they proved that his penicillin worked.*

with the deadly *Streptococcus* bacteria, and then gave them Chain's new, purer penicillin. The mice recovered. When Florey returned, Chain showed him what he had done. At last Florey was convinced that Chain was on to something good. He arranged for further tests on many more mice. Had it just been luck the first time? Somewhat to his surprise, the experiments were successful. Chain had proved that penicillin could kill bacteria without harming the subject taking it.

BELOW: A scientist tests solutions of penicillin during the Second World War.

THE ALBERT ALEXANDER TRIAL

By now the Second World War was raging. All Britain's resources were being used to support the war effort. Many people remembered the terrible First World War and how men died in their thousands from infected wounds and gangrene. There had never been a greater need for treatment of bacterial infection than there was at this time.

In 1941 a 48-year-old policeman called Albert Alexander was brought to the Radcliffe Infirmary hospital in Oxford. He had cut his face while shaving and a nasty infection had broken out. *Staphylococcus* and *Streptococcus* bacteria had taken hold and infected his

ABOVE: *Photographed in the 1940s, these stacks of glass trays are growing penicillin cultures. The cultures are kept sterile and then injected with* Penicillium notatum. *Around ten days later, a penicillin-rich fungus is produced. Later in the process liquid penicillin is created, from which a penicillin salt is extracted. It was a time-consuming process and did not produce enough of the drug to keep Albert Alexander alive.*

face, eyes and lungs with septicaemia, in which bacteria poison the blood and use it to carry infection to other parts of the body. Alexander had a very high fever and was close to death.

His doctor, Charles Fletcher, had heard about Florey and Chain's work and knew of the desperate need to try the new penicillin out on people rather than just laboratory animals. He figured that since Alexander was dying, he would have nothing to lose in trying it out. With time running out, Alexander was injected with penicillin. To begin with the results seemed almost miraculous – his temperature dropped and the infection began to clear.

But just when things were going so well, Fletcher had a serious setback: he ran out of penicillin. It was difficult enough for Florey's team to make enough penicillin to continue their research, let alone have any to spare for human trials – the type of mould they were using did not grow quickly enough. The research team desperately tried to grow more penicillin to help clear Alexander's infection completely, and when they realised this was not working, they even tried extracting any unused penicillin that Alexander passed out in his urine. Sadly, it was not enough. The bacteria in Alexander's body took hold again, and he died.

FURTHER SUCCESSES – AND ONE BIG PROBLEM

Although Albert Alexander's death was a tragedy, and a setback for the scientists and doctors who were hoping this would be the breakthrough case, the trial nonetheless proved that penicillin worked. Further experiments were conducted. Two boys, aged four and 15, and an 84-year-old man were all cured of blood poisoning. When he heard what Florey and Chain had achieved, Fleming himself went to them and asked if he could have some penicillin to treat a friend of his who was suffering from a serious infection. Once again, the penicillin worked and Fleming's friend was cured. This case made it into the newspapers, and more and more people, including scientists, became aware of the fact that penicillin could save lives.

This was, of course, good news, but the key problem remained – it was all very well treating a handful of subjects, but how could they make penicillin on a scale that would answer the great need for such a wonderful drug?

Fact

WARTIME MEASURES
Because they were working at the height of the Second World War, Florey, Chain and rest of the team were very worried about what would happen to their research if Britain was invaded by the Germans. They had come a long way and did not want all their hard work to be lost, so they took extreme measures to prevent this. They smeared samples of the mould they were researching into the linings of their coats. Once there it could survive for a long time as long as it was kept dry. This way, they hoped, in the event of an invasion, at least one of them might be able to escape and continue their research in a safer country.

Key People

Howard Florey (1898–1968) was born in Australia. He completed his medical studies in England and the United States. By 1931 he was Professor of Pathology at Sheffield University. Florey had a very distinguished medical career, but he will always be best known for his work with Ernst Chain on penicillin. Florey was knighted in 1944 and shared the Nobel Prize for Medicine in 1945 with Ernst Chain and Alexander Fleming. In 1960 he was made President of the Royal Society in London, a society for scientists, founded by King Charles II in 1660.

CHAPTER FOUR

'There is the danger that the ignorant man may easily underdose himself and, by exposing his microbes to non-lethal quantities of the drug, make them resistant.' ALEXANDER FLEMING

Penicillin for All

ABOVE: *During the Second World War, women worked in the factories doing jobs usually carried out by the men who were away fighting. Helping to make penicillin for the soldiers was one of these jobs.*

BELOW: *These scientists in America in 1943 are refining, or purifying, the penicillin to make sure it is free from impurities.*

BY MID-1941 BRITAIN HAD REACHED A crisis point in the war. German submarines sank many ships carrying food and supplies from the United States and Canada to Britain. In Britain there were no resources to spare for medical research into penicillin, even though this was a time when a cure for bacterial infection was so desperately needed.

THE PENICILLIN TEAM

Florey made the dangerous trip across the Atlantic to seek help in the USA. America had huge financial resources, many highly skilled scientists, and was, for the time being at least, safe from the threat of enemy attack.

Florey and his Oxford colleague Norman Heatley went to the Northern Regional Research Laboratory in Peoria, Illinois, in the summer of 1941. Heatley had developed techniques for separating penicillin from the mould without inactivating it. He found that hospital bed-pans were just the right shape to grow the penicillin!

A team was assembled at Peoria and started work in July 1941. Many people were involved, but some of the most important were Robert Coghill, in charge of the fermentation division, O. E. May, George Ward, Kenneth Raper and Andrew Moyer. Moyer suggested using a liquid extracted from maize, a common food crop, to grow the mould. In the American Midwest, where there were millions of acres of farmland, this maize extract was easy to come by, as well as cheap.

The next problem was getting hold of the *Penicillium* spores to begin the growing process. *Penicillium notatum*, which Fleming had discovered and Florey and Chain had been using, did not grow quickly or in abundance,

BELOW: *The team assembled at the laboratory at Peoria in the US during the war became known as 'the Superpenicillin Team'. Their great teamwork was responsible for the mass-production of the drug, which saved many thousands of lives.*

RIGHT: These flasks are growing penicillin cultures. In 1943, when this picture was taken, the team at Peoria were on the verge of finding the best mould from which to make penicillin.

Fact

THE CANTALOUPE MELON
The team at Peoria had been trying for some time to find the right mould to grow the penicillin, and it was one of the Peoria laboratory staff who solved the problem in 1943. Mary Hunt brought in a cantaloupe melon which had a gold-coloured mould growing on it. This turned out to be a new type of 'Penicillium'. It was called 'Penicillium chrysogenum', or 'golden penicillin'.

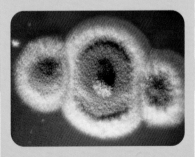

ABOVE: A fungal culture of Penicillium chrysogenum, *which proved to produce the most penicillin of all the cultures the Peoria team experimented on. The golden ring around the edge gave it its nickname, 'golden penicillin'.*

so they decided to try to find another type of *Penicillium* mould that would have the same effect on bacteria. Soil samples from many sources were tried in Peoria. A mould that grew on a cantaloupe melon turned out to be the best source.

MASS-PRODUCTION

The new mould produced 200 times more penicillin than the old form. Now there was a glimmer of hope that large quantities of penicillin could be made. The Peoria team began to refine the mould to make it yield even more penicillin and by the time they had finished, it could make 1,000 times as much as Fleming's original type. So, the team now had a mould that produced a high quantity of penicillin. Their next challenge was to create large enough quantities of the mould itself to help the soldiers who were dying of infection in the theatres of war.

The biggest step towards mass-production was made by the US company Pfizer. They bought a redundant ice factory and installed new equipment to make penicillin. They used huge tanks, kept sterile by pumping air through them (*Penicillium* needs lots of air to grow), and found that they could produce much larger amounts of the drug. It was brilliantly successful and mass-production of penicillin, the first of the drugs we now call antibiotics, was possible for the first time.

Fact

PENICILLIN IN THE SECOND WORLD WAR

As soon as a way was found to mass-produce penicillin, the drug was packaged and dispatched to the soldiers. The Allied troops who landed in France in 1944 carried penicillin with them. In the first half of 1943 only about 80 million units of penicillin had been made each month. By the end of the Second World War, production had rocketed to 650 billion units a month.

ABOVE: *Cases such as this, containing penicillin and the apparatus for administering it, were given to soldiers to carry during the last year of the Second World War.*

THE WONDER DRUG

During the war, most of the production of penicillin was given over to supplying the armed forces in Europe and Asia. Only when the war ended in 1945 did penicillin become available for civilians.

Using 135,000 soil samples from around the world, Pfizer carried out 20 million tests to try to improve the production of penicillin. By this stage they were also trying to create other antibiotics. They produced a new antibiotic they called terramycin (*terra* is Latin for 'soil').

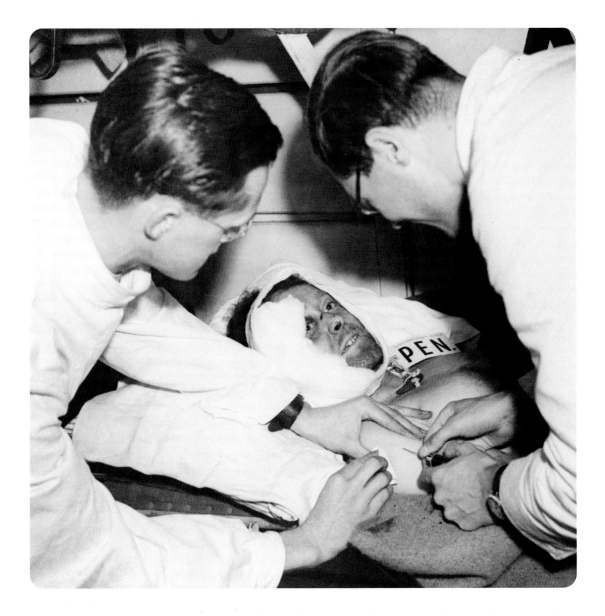

ABOVE: In the last few months of the Second World War, army medics were supplied with penicillin. There is no doubt it saved thousands of lives. Here the medics administer penicillin to a wounded British soldier.

Lots of scientists jumped on the bandwagon and it was not long before other antibiotics became available. Some of these even killed bacteria on which penicillin had no effect. These included streptomycin, which was made from a mould discovered in 1944 called *Streptomyces griseus*. It is used to treat tuberculosis. Chloramphenicol was discovered in 1947 and used to treat typhoid fever and salmonella. In 1949 penicillin was successfully used to kill bacteria that had been contaminating virus samples that were used to produce a polio vaccine.

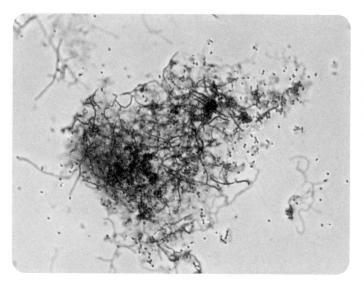

LEFT: Streptomyces bacteria are found in some types of soil. In 1944, scientists discovered that Streptomyces produced their own antibacterial agents that could treat tuberculosis. Today, more efficient drugs for this disease are used, but at the time it was considered a significant breakthrough.

NOBEL PRIZES

Although penicillin could not kill all bacteria, it had opened the door to all sorts of new research. In 1944 Fleming and Florey were knighted in England. In 1939 Domagk had won the Nobel Prize for Medicine for his work on sulphonamides. In 1945, Florey and Chain shared the Nobel Prize for Medicine with Alexander Fleming.

BELOW: Alexander Fleming's amazing discovery won him the Nobel Prize in 1945. He shared the prize with Howard Florey and Ernst Chain.

In a speech at the banquet to celebrate the Nobel Prize, Fleming said he knew luck had played a part in his discovery, and acknowledged what Florey and Chain had done to make penicillin work. It had been teamwork that had made the difference.

Chain said he was 'profoundly grateful to Providence' for the part he had been able to play in helping to reduce the suffering of soldiers in the Second World War. Both he and Florey contrasted the wonderful teamwork that led to the discovery and production of penicillin with the terrible state of the world in 1945. They hoped that penicillin would play a part in a new and more hopeful future.

CHAPTER FIVE

'It is time to close the book on infectious diseases and pay more attention to chronic ailments.' WILLIAM H. STEWART, US SURGEON-GENERAL

Penicillin Today

ABOVE: *These are DNA plasmids from the bacteria* E. coli. *Plasmids are a problem in the success of penicillin, because they can replicate independently and travel from one cell to another, making those cells resistant.*

BELOW: *The bacteria* Staphylococcus pyogenes *(light brown). The area to the left of the dish is where the bacteria has developed a resistance to penicillin (the black circle around the white dot).*

FLEMING, FLOREY, CHAIN AND ALL THE other scientists had achieved something extraordinary. Penicillin and the other new antibiotics not only offered treatment for many infections, but also changed the way in which medicine was practised.

AN INFECTION-FREE FUTURE?

After mass-production of penicillin began, people believed that they had conquered infectious diseases once and for all, and in 1969 the Surgeon-General of the United States, William H. Stewart, told Congress that infectious diseases had been vanquished. He was wrong.

It was not long before scientists noticed several serious problems with antibiotics. To begin with, they did not work for everybody – some patients were allergic to them. Other, far more serious issues arose as scientists learned more about bacteria. They realised that they could reproduce very quickly. Scientists also learned that bacteria can mutate, or change; such changes can make an organism stronger or weaker.

Mutation can be seen as a good thing – it is probably these changes in our bodies that have brought us to where we are today. But human mutation is very, very slow. It takes thousands of years and many generations for a mutated 'good' gene to become one that most people share. Bacteria reproduce so rapidly that those with mutated genes occur far more often and replicate themselves with exceptional speed. Scientists realised that it was only a matter of time before bacteria mutated into forms that the new antibiotics could not kill.

More importantly, bacteria can transfer genes that make them resistant to each other. Plasmids pass from one bacterium to another, carrying the power of resistance with them. This means that even bacteria that have never been exposed to antibiotics are already resistant to them. The worst thing about this is that once bacteria are resistant to an antibiotic, the change is permanent.

BELOW: *There are several ways in which bacteria can become resistant to antibiotics like penicillin.*

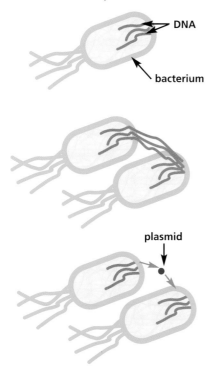

DNA

bacterium

plasmid

SPONTANEOUS MUTATION: *The genetic material in the bacteria (DNA) can change spontaneously.*

TRANSFORMATION: *One bacterium can pass on DNA to another bacterium – including its resistance to antibiotics.*

PLASMID RESISTANCE: *A small particle of DNA called a plasmid can move from one type of bacterium to another, taking different resistances with it.*

Fact

SUPERBUGS

In 1952 'Staphylococcus' was one of the types of bacterium that could be killed by penicillin. Many people have 'Staphylococcus' in their noses, and it is harmless there, but if it gets into the bloodstream it can cause serious problems, especially if someone is already weakened from another illness.

Within a few years, 'Staphylococcus' had become resistant to penicillin and other penicillin-based antibiotics. The new type of bacteria was named 'methicillin-resistant Staphylococcus aureus', more commonly known as MRSA, and was nicknamed the 'superbug'. Eventually only an antibiotic called vancomycin could kill it and cure the patient. Vancomycin is not an antibiotic that doctors like using because it has many side-effects – but they often have no choice.

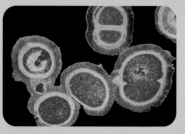

ABOVE: *A deadly cluster of MRSA, a strain of bacteria that has turned out to be resistant to most forms of antibiotic. This is one of the 'superbugs'.*

Fact

DNA AND MUTATION

All living organisms, including humans, have the genetic code of DNA. It is the DNA in genes that makes eyes brown or blue, hair dark or fair, and so on. It can also give resistance to disease. DNA has to keep copying itself, but sometimes this goes wrong and the copy is not exact. This can happen when a baby is growing inside its mother, and the baby is then born with a mutated gene. Usually a mutated gene weakens the organism, but sometimes it can bring a great advantage, like resistance to a disease. When that happens, those with the stronger genes are more likely to survive. Scientists call this 'selection'.

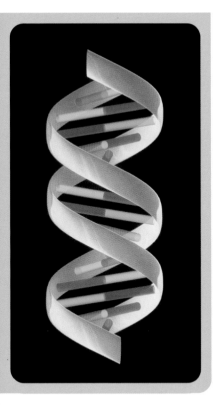

RIGHT: The twisted double helix of a DNA strand contains the 'code for life' – everything that makes us individuals. Sometimes things go wrong when DNA replicates itself, and a mutated gene is created.

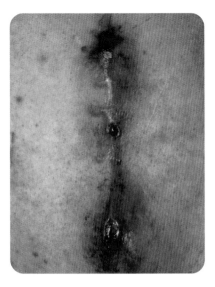

BELOW: Despite doctors' best efforts, disease still spreads in hospitals, which are warm and full of bacteria; these can cause all sorts of infections if they get into open wounds. The redness around the scar here probably indicates that an infection has taken hold.

WHAT WENT WRONG?

Bacteria like *Staphylococcus* thrive in hospitals. There are lots of people with infections, wounds and injuries where the bacteria can enter the body, and hospitals are warm. These make ideal conditions for bacteria to spread. Today, about 400,000 patients a year in US hospitals catch an infection while they are there, and about a quarter of them die from 'superbugs' and other bacterial infections. In the United Kingdom at least 5,000 people die every year from superbug infections.

Why has this happened? Fleming had known that administering the correct dosage of penicillin was very important – there had to be enough to kill every single infected bacterium in the patient's body. If not, some of the bacteria would survive and have time to mutate into penicillin-resistant types. When antibiotics were introduced the public and even doctors were so excited that they used them whenever they could. When people felt better, they often stopped taking the

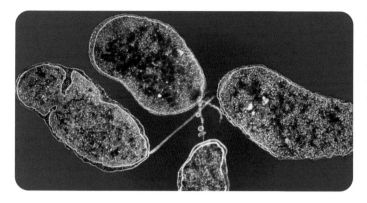

LEFT: Through a powerful microscope, scientists can study bacterial behaviour. These Vibrio cholerae bacteria, which cause the disease cholera, are exchanging DNA in the process known as conjugation.

antibiotics, so some bacteria survived and mutated into resistant forms. Doctors often gave antibiotics even when they were not needed, believing that they would help prevent disease breaking out.

OTHER PROBLEMS

Penicillin and some other antibiotics kill useful bacteria in the body. Sometimes this allows harmful bacteria, which had been previously unable to do any damage, a chance to cause disease.

Antibiotics have also been given to animals, sometimes because they were ill, but more often to prevent disease. One estimate is that more than two-thirds of all the antibiotics available have been routinely given to animals. These antibiotics end up in our food. Today a form of salmonella, a disease-causing bacterium that is resistant to antibiotics, is often found in milk, meat and eggs.

All this means that bacteria have been coming into contact with antibiotics far more often than they should have. Every time bacteria meet an antibiotic there is a chance some will survive and develop a resistant type that the antibiotic cannot kill, and then pass it on to other bacteria.

NEW USES OF ANTIBIOTICS

Despite all the problems that arose after the discovery of penicillin, we should not underestimate how important antibiotics were, and still are. Penicillin has been significant not just in saving lives, but also in

Fact

DETROIT VRSA

In 1997 the news that everyone in the medical world dreaded was announced: a new type of 'Staphylococcus aureus' bacteria had turned up in Japan, and the antibiotic doctors relied on – vancomycin – could not kill it. This type is called 'vancomycin-resistant Staphylococcus aureus', or VRSA, a 'superbug'.

A Detroit woman came to hospital. She had sores on her feet that would not clear up, even though she took lots of antibiotics. In April 2002 doctors had to cut off one of her toes to try to stop the infection. That was when they discovered she was infected with a type of 'Staphylococcus' that cannot be killed by vancomycin. The woman was successfully treated with other antibiotics, but since then 'Staphylococcus aureus' has become resistant to some of them, too.

RIGHT: *Today penicillin is created from man-made materials rather than being produced from natural substances like mould. These are crystals of penicillin made from potassium salt.*

BELOW: *Hospital technicians studying bacteria samples from patients. It is important to know which bacteria are causing a particular infection, so that the most suitable antibiotic can be used in treatment.*

laying the foundations for new research into killing bacteria. A whole family of penicillin-based antibiotics has been developed. They are easy to spot because their names always end in -cillin, and they all work in the same way – by stopping the bacteria from making cell walls. Examples of penicillin-type antibiotics are amoxicillin and ampicillin. Both are used to treat infections, such as ear infections, infections after surgery or urinary infections. Today, they are no longer produced from natural substances like mould, but can be created artificially.

But superbugs are making doctors think again about antibiotics. Scientists are looking for new methods to attack bacteria. The plan is to try to use antibiotics as little as possible, especially if the disease is not life-threatening, to keep accurate records of

Fact

BACTERIOPHAGES

Just like animals, bacteria have natural enemies. These are viruses called bacteriophages. Viruses attack cells, and different viruses like different organisms. Viruses need resources from cells to reproduce. This normally damages or destroys the cells, and that is exactly what happens to a bacterium when a bacteriophage attacks it. Today, scientists around the world are trying to see whether bacteriophages can be used to kill disease-causing bacteria.

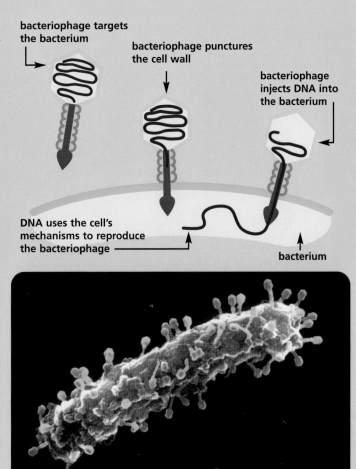

bacteriophage targets the bacterium

bacteriophage punctures the cell wall

bacteriophage injects DNA into the bacterium

DNA uses the cell's mechanisms to reproduce the bacteriophage

bacterium

RIGHT: *Viruses known as bacteriophages are present in the human body. They fight bacteria by attacking their cell walls and injecting DNA into the bacteria. Here, bacteriophages (blue) attack an* E coli *bacterium cell (brown).*

what antibiotics are used and where, and to use exactly the right antibiotic in the correct amounts.

Penicillin is still at the forefront of the battle against infection. Bacteria fight back against penicillin by producing a special enzyme that changes the penicillin molecules and makes them harmless. To counteract this, some researchers are experimenting with a new type of penicillin that attacks as soon as the bacteria try to make the penicillin harmless.

The bacterium that causes diphtheria contains a part that renders it harmless. That part is called a toxin-repressor and occurs naturally in the bacterium. In certain cases the toxin-repressor is defeated and the

ABOVE: *Some people are allergic to penicillin, or have an infection caused by bacteria that are resistant to penicillin, so other drugs have been developed. Among these are the 'macrolide' drugs, which can treat bacterial infections when penicillin will not work.*

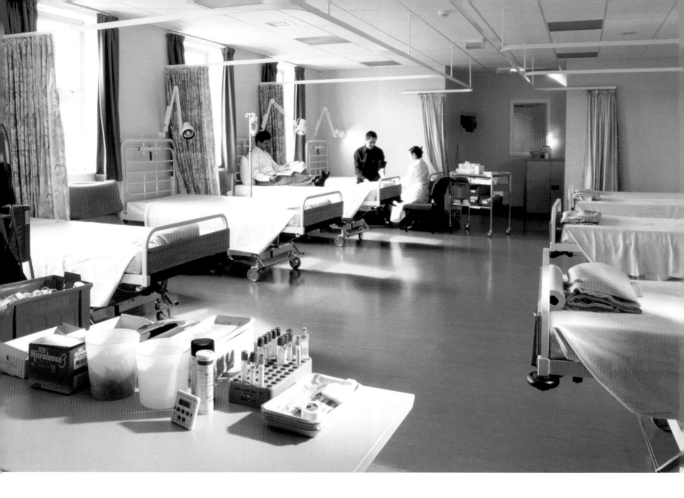

bacterium becomes dangerous. So when the bacterium enters a person who does not have enough iron in his or her bloodstream, the toxin-repressor falls off, the toxins are activated and cause diphtheria. Finding a way to stop the toxin-repressor falling off could help prevent the disease taking hold.

FIGHTING BACTERIA

Changing behaviour is at the heart of fighting bacteria. In December 2003 the British government announced a campaign to improve standards of hospital hygiene. Washing hands and sterilising equipment more thoroughly, and disinfecting floors more frequently can reduce the spread of bacteria.

Scientists and doctors are also learning more about the nature of disease itself. For example, antibiotics help treat cholera, but they only make recovery faster. Cholera causes diarrhoea and it is the loss of water and salt that makes it dangerous. By the early 1900s it was found that deaths could be reduced from 50 to five per cent just by giving patients water and salt. Even more significant has been improved sanitation, which stops the disease being transmitted in the first place.

One estimate is that as many as one-third of all antibiotic treatments is unnecessary. Only when the infection will not go away ('persistent') or is spreading ('systemic') do antibiotics have to be used. Another possible solution is to use antibiotics only in the very part of the body they are needed. A Seattle-based team has been working on an antibiotic cream to treat foot ulcers. That way, the antibiotic does not get into the rest of the body. Neither of these solutions will stop bacteria becoming resistant, but it will take longer for them to do so.

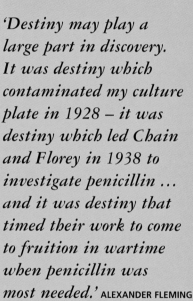

'*Destiny may play a large part in discovery. It was destiny which contaminated my culture plate in 1928 – it was destiny which led Chain and Florey in 1938 to investigate penicillin ... and it was destiny that timed their work to come to fruition in wartime when penicillin was most needed.*' ALEXANDER FLEMING

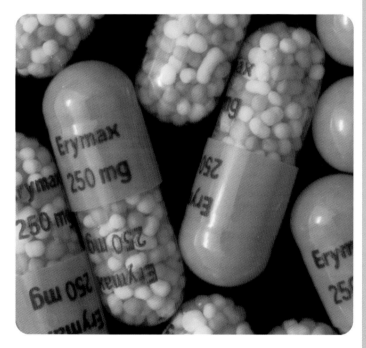

WHAT DOES THE FUTURE HOLD?

The battle against bacteria is very far from won. But the work done by Fleming, Florey and Chain, and all the other brilliant scientists who brought penicillin to the world in the 1940s, showed what medical science could do. They paved the way for today's research. Fleming put it down to teamwork and destiny, and that is what will help us continue the battle against bacteria.

TIMELINE

1683	Anton van Leeuwenhoek first describes bacteria
1848	The first Public Health Act is passed in England
1854	John Snow proves that contaminated water can cause cholera
1861	Louis Pasteur discovers that micro-organisms can cause decay; Prince Albert dies of typhoid fever
1876	John Tyndall observes the effect of *Penicillium* mould on bacteria
1883	Robert Koch identifies the cholera bacterium
1909	Paul Ehrlich discovers 'magic bullet' drugs to kill bacteria
1911	*Penicillium* mould is first described by Richard Westling
1921	Alexander Fleming discovers lysozyme
1925	André Gratia and Sarah Dath observe *Penicillium*'s ability to kill bacteria
1928	Fleming accidentally discovers that *Penicillium* mould kills certain bacteria; he records and preserves the evidence
1929	Fleming publishes his work and establishes the name 'penicillin' for the active ingredient
1935	Bacteria-killing sulphonamide drugs are discovered by Gerhard Domagk
1938	Howard Florey and Ernst Chain start work on penicillin at Oxford
1939	Domagk is awarded the Nobel Prize for Medicine
1941	Penicillin is tried out on Albert Alexander; research moves to Peoria, USA
1943	*Penicillium chrysogenum* is discovered on the cantaloupe melon
1944	Penicillin is refined and enough is produced to be used in Second World War
1945	Fleming, Florey and Chain share the Nobel Prize for Medicine
c. 1955	*Staphylococcus* bacteria become resistant to penicillin; the emergence of MRSA superbugs follows
1969	William H. Stewart, Surgeon-General of the USA, announces (wrongly) that infectious diseases have been conquered
1997	Vancomycin-resistant *Staphylococcus aureus* (VRSA) appears in Japan
2003	The British government announces a hygiene campaign to rid hospitals of MRSA and VRSA
2004	Cases of syphilis increase, as an antibiotic-resistant strain develops

GLOSSARY

AGAR A jelly-like substance on which cultures can be easily grown.

ANTIBODY Produced by white blood cells to attack invaders like bacteria or viruses.

ANTIGEN A protein that an organism recognises as being a foreign protein.

BACTERIOPHAGE A virus that attacks bacteria.

BINARY FISSION Reproduction by dividing into two.

BOWEL The intestine; a long tube from the stomach that finishes the digestion process; also called the gut.

CHOLERA An infection of the intestine, usually caused by contaminated food or water.

CHROMOSOME A thread-like structure consisting of genetic units (genes) made of DNA in a cell nucleus. Bacterial DNA forms the nucleoid, as bacteria do not have nuclei.

CONJUGATION The process by which plasmids are passed from one bacterium to another.

CULTURES Collections of microbes that have been cultivated in a laboratory.

CYTOPLASM The material that makes up the part of a cell that is not the nucleus.

DNA Deoxyribonucleic acid; a long molecule made from four bases. DNA is the nucleic acid in which genetic information is coded.

ENZYME A protein that acts as a catalyst (something that influences a reaction but does not become part it) for biochemical reactions.

EUKARYOTIC Relating to an organism with a well-defined nucleus.

FERMENTATION The process of chemical change caused by micro-organisms.

GANGRENE The death of body tissue after it has been attacked by bacteria.

GENE A length of DNA. Thousands of genes together make a chromosome.

HAEMORRHAGE When bleeding occurs unexpectedly, too profusely to be stopped.

IMMUNE SYSTEM The collection of cells and proteins that work to protect the body from harmful micro-organisms.

LYMPHOCYTES White blood cells that produce antibodies to destroy bacteria.

LYSOZYME A substance produced by living matter that kills some bacteria, but not those that cause disease.

METABOLISM The sum of all the chemical and physical changes that occur in living organisms, resulting in growth, production of energy, etc.

MICROBE A micro-organism that can only be seen using a microscope.

MRSA Methicillin-resistant *Staphylococcus aureus*; a superbug that is resistant to penicillin-based antibiotics, and is now becoming resistant to others, too

MUCUS Liquid that helps protect membranes, particularly in the nose and gut.

MUTATION When DNA produces a copy that is not exact. The changed DNA may have advantages or disadvantages.

NUCLEOID The DNA-containing structure of prokaryotic cells; not bounded by a membrane.

PATHOGEN A bacterium that causes disease.

PATHOLOGY The study of the causes and effects of disease.

PHAGOCYTES White blood cells that engulf and destroy bacteria.

PLASMID A ring of DNA in a cell that can replicate independently within a bacterium.

PROKARYOTIC Relating to lower organisms with no well-defined nucleus, e.g. bacteria.

PROTEIN Required for the structure, function and regulation of the body's cells, tissues and organs; each protein has unique functions.

RESISTANT Unaffected by antibiotic drugs.

RIBOSOME The part of a cell that makes proteins.

RNA Ribonucleic acid; the information encoded in DNA is translated into messenger RNA, which controls the synthesis of new proteins.

SIDE-EFFECT An additional or unwanted effect caused by some drugs.

SULPHONAMIDES Bacteria-killing drugs developed in the 1930s. Sulphonamides are very effective in killing bacteria but have unpleasant side-effects.

SUPERBUG A bacterium that cannot be killed by normal antibiotics.

SYMPTOM A sign of illness – an indicator that the body is not working properly.

TOXIN REPRESSOR The part of certain bacteria, such as diphtheria bacteria, which renders it harmless.

VIRULENT Extremely harmful; the diseases caused by the superbugs are virulent.

VIRUS A parasitic micro-organism; a piece of nucleic acid (DNA or RNA) wrapped in a thin coat of protein. Viruses are unable to live independently, using resources of living cells to reproduce and grow, thereby causing disease. They are unaffected by antibiotics.

VITAMIN A substance essential in small quantities for the normal functioning of metabolism in the body.

VRSA Vancomycin-resistant *Staphylococcus aureus*; a superbug that is resistant to penicillin-based antibiotics.

WHITE BLOOD CELLS Cells in the blood that are responsible for destroying harmful bacteria, viruses and fungi.

FURTHER INFORMATION

WEB SITES

www.timelinescience.org/resource/students/penicilin/penicilin.htm
A good resource for students wanting to find out more about the germ theory of medicine and the rise of antibiotics, with information about Fleming, Florey, Chain and others who contributed to the great discovery.

www.schoolshistory.org.uk/infectiousdisease.htm
A great revision site created by teachers, broken down into easy-to-use sections and including information on Fleming, Florey and Chain as well as quizzes, questions and links.

There are also many sites offering biographies of the key people involved in the development of antibiotics, and brief histories of the discovery of penicillin. A search will reveal a lot of fascinating information.

BOOKS

Alexander Fleming and the Story of Penicillin by John Bankston: Unlocking the Secrets of Science, Mitchell Lane Publishers, 2001
Alexander Fleming by Richard Tames: Life Times, Franklin Watts, 2003
Antibiotics by Evelyn B. Kelly: Great Medical Discoveries, Lucent Books, 2003
Howard Florey: Miracle Maker by Kirsty Murray: Allen & Unwin Children's Books, 1999
Penicillin: A Breakthrough in Medicine by Richard Tames: Heinemann Library, 2001
The Mould in Dr Florey's Coat: How Penicillin Began the Age of Miracle Cures by Eric Lax: Little Brown, 2004

OTHER SOURCES

Medical science changes rapidly, and new antibiotics are being developed all the time to deal with diseases and to address the problem of antibiotic-resistant strains. Keep an eye out in the newspapers and on the Internet for news stories about these developments.

INDEX